CONTENTS

LOGOTRON LOGO – GLOSSARY OF COMMANDS

BG   returns background colour

BK *number*   moves turtle backwards *number* of steps

CLEAN   clears graphics area of screen

CS   clears screen and centres turtle

EDALL   finds all procedures in the editor

END   shows end of procedure definition

ER *procedure name*   erases named procedure from working memory

ERALL   erases all procedures from working memory

FENCE   stops turtle going off the screen

FD *number*   moves turtle forward *number* of steps

HT   hides turtle

IF *a[list1] [list2]*   if *a* is true then *list1* is executed, if *a* is false then *list2* is executed (optional), for example
                              IF: LENGTH>20[SETPC 4] [SETPC 7]

LT *number*   turns turtle to the left by the angle specified by the *number*

LOAD *file name*   loads all procedures in the named file

OP *object*   returns control to calling procedure with *object* as output, for example
                              To SQUARE :N
                              OP :N*:N
                              END

PC   returns current pencolour

PD   puts turtle's pen down

PE   erases lines over which turtle passes

POALL   prints out definitions of all the procedures in working memory

POS   returns the coordinates of the turtle's position as a list

PRINT *expression*   prints *expression* which can be a number, a word or a list

PU   lifts turtle's pen up

RANDOM *integer*   returns a random number between 0 and *integer*

REPEAT *integer* [list]   repeats a list a number of times specified by the *integer*

RT *number*   moves turtle to the right by the angle specified by *number*

SAVE *file name*   saves all the procedures in the named file

SETBG *number*   changes background colour to colour specified by *number*

SETH *number*   changes turtle's heading to an angle specified by *number*

SETPC *number*   changes pen colour to colour specified by *number*

SETPOS *[x,y]*   changes turtle's position to the coordinates specified by *x* and *y*

SETX *number*   moves turtle's *x* coordinate to the coordinate specified by *number*

SETY *number*   moves turtle's *y* coordinate to the coordinate specified by *number*

TS   allows the whole screen to be used for text

UNWALK *procedure name*   cancels the effect of WALK

WALK *procedure name*   helps you to debug your procedure

WINDOW   lets the turtle go outside the screen

WRAP   makes the turtle wrap around the screen

XCOR   returns turtle's *x* coordinate

YCOR   returns turtle's *y* coordinate

BEGINNING LOGO COMMANDS

Turtle Geometry 1

Try out these Logo turtle commands.

Draw a picture using only these commands.

FD   *Any number*

BK   *Any number*

        RT   *Any number*

        LT   *Any number*

© R. Sutherland **LogoPack 1** *Century Maths*
Stanley Thornes (Publishers) Ltd 1991

Turtle Geometry 2

Some more useful turtle commands.

CLEAN Short for clearing the graphics area of the screen

CS Short for clearscreen

PU Short for penup

PD Short for pendown

ST Short for showturtle

HT Short for hideturtle

> *You can check the meaning of PE with your teacher*

PE Short for penerase

To find out how to use PE try

BBC	**Nimbus**
FD 140	FD 140
PE	PE
BK 140	BK 140
PD	SETPC 1
FD 50	FD 50

© R. Sutherland **LogoPack 1** *Century Maths*
Stanley Thornes (Publishers) Ltd 1991

B3

Logo People

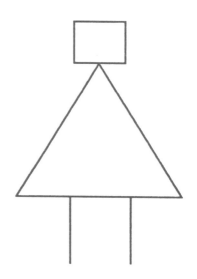

Design your own Logo person.

BEGINNING LOGO COMMANDS

Logo Challenge

Choose one of the following Logo challenges.

Keep a record of your commands.

1. Design anything you like using only the FD and RT commands.

2. Design anything you like using only the BK and LT command.

3. Design anything you like using FD and BK and turtle turns between 90 and 180 degrees.

4. Design anything you like using FD and BK and turtle turns between 180 and 270 degrees.

In all the challenges you are also allowed to use

PU
PD
PE

© R. Sutherland   **LogoPack 1**   *Century Maths*
Stanley Thornes (Publishers) Ltd 1991

PROCEDURES

Defining and Editing a Procedure

A procedure is a set of Logo commands with its own name.

First work out the commands which you want to name
(for example, the commands to draw a tree).

Choose a name for your procedure, for example TREE.

Then type:

EDIT [TREE]

This takes you into the Logo editor.

```
TO  TREE


←

END
```

Type your
commands here.

To get out of the editor
- press Ctrl and C on the **BBC** or
- press Esc on the **Nimbus**

When you are out of the editor, type:

TREE
FD 50
TREE

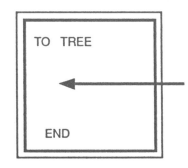

Use your procedure TREE
to make a new pattern.

You can EDIT your procedure when it does not do what you want it to do.

For example, if you wanted to edit your procedure called TREE, type

EDIT [TREE]

This takes you into the Logo editor.

```
TO  TREE


←

END
```

Change the commands in
your procedure by using
the arrow keys to move up
and down and along the
lines, and the delete key.

To get out of the editor
- press Ctrl and C on the **BBC** or
- press Esc on the **Nimbus**

Other useful commands:

EDALL	Finds all procedures in the editor.
ER [list of names of procedures]	Erases named procedures from working memory.
ERALL	Erases all procedures from working memory.
POALL	Prints out definitions of all procedures in the working memory.

© R. Sutherland **LogoPack 1** *Century Maths*
Stanley Thornes (Publishers) Ltd 1991

Moving Procedures About

Write a procedure to draw a flower and a procedure to draw a tree.

```
TO FLOWER



END
```

! *Make sure that the turtle starts and finishes in the same place.*

```
TO TREE



END
```

Write a procedure to move your TREE and FLOWER about the screen.

> Try
> TREE
> RT 90 PU FD 100 LT 90 PD
> FLOWER

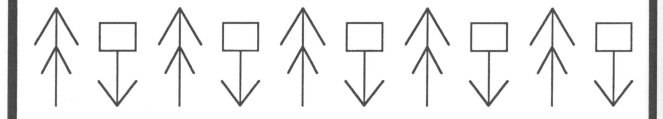

© R. Sutherland **LogoPack 1** *Century Maths*
Stanley Thornes (Publishers) Ltd 1991

PROCEDURES

Saving and Loading Procedures

You can SAVE your procedures in a file on your computer disk.

1. Choose a filename, for example JOANN1

2. Check that your disk is in the disk drive.

3. Type

! *You can use no more than 7 characters for the filename.*

SAVE " JOANN1

ALL your procedures are now saved in the file called JOANN1

You can LOAD your procedures from your file called JOANN1

1. Check that your disk is in the disk drive.

2. Type

LOAD " JOANN1

ALL the procedures in the file called JOANN1 have now been read into the computer memory.

! *You will need to check the precise syntax for your RML Nimbus system.*

© R. Sutherland **LogoPack 1** *Century Maths*
Stanley Thornes (Publishers) Ltd 1991

PROCEDURES

Earring Designs

Design an earring.
Write a procedure for your design.

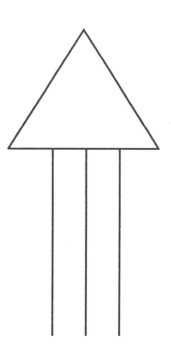

PROCEDURES

Movement

You can create the effect of movement
by drawing a line and then rubbing it out.

If you have a **BBC** machine, try typing:

REPEAT 12 [FD 100 PE BK 100 RT 30 PD]

If you have a **Nimbus** machine, try typing:

REPEAT 12 [FD 100 PE BK 100 RT 30 SETPC 1]

Use this idea to design a
procedure for a

Clock with moving pointers

or a

Person running

or a

Dog with a wagging tail

or a

Flicker book

© R. Sutherland **LogoPack 1** *Century Maths*
Stanley Thornes (Publishers) Ltd 1991

Useful Pen and Screen Commands

WRAP   This makes the turtle wrap around the screen

FENCE   This fences the turtle in the screen area

WINDOW   This lets the turtle go outside the screen

SETPC   *Whole number*   Sets the pencolour

SETBG   *Whole number*   Sets the background colour

PC   Returns the pencolour

BG   Returns the background colour

© R. Sutherland **LogoPack 1** *Century Maths*
Stanley Thornes (Publishers) Ltd 1991

The REPEAT Command

REPEAT   *Any whole number*   [Commands to be repeated]

For example

REPEAT 6 [RT 30 FD 50 RT 120 FD 50 LT 150]

Use the REPEAT command to make a border pattern.

© R. Sutherland   **LogoPack 1**   *Century Maths*
Stanley Thornes (Publishers) Ltd 1991

SUPERPROCEDURES

Building Up

Write a procedure to
draw a letter T.

```
TO   TEE



END
```

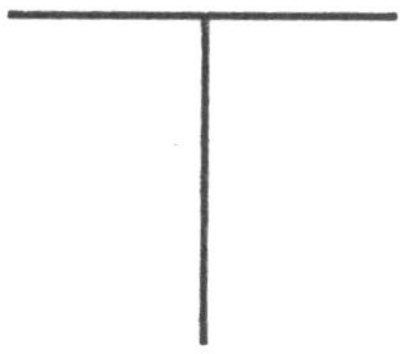

Try out some commands to make
an interesting pattern

TEE RT 60
TEE RT 60
TEE RT 60 . . .

```
TO PATTERN
TEE  RT 60
TEE  RT 60
TEE  RT 60
TEE  RT 60
TEE  RT 60
TEE  RT 60
END
```

Put these commands in
a procedure called
PATTERN

Now type:

PATTERN

SUPERPROCEDURES

Breaking Down

Take a pattern

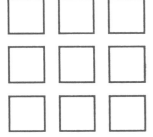

Study this pattern and *break* it *down* into parts.

You will need to:

● decide on the part

● write a procedure to draw the part

For this pattern you could write a procedure to draw a square.

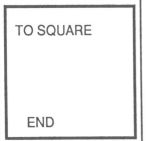

TO SQUARE

END

!
■

Think about where you want the turtle to start and end in your procedure.

> Looks like a load of squares to me.

Then write a superprocedure to draw the pattern.

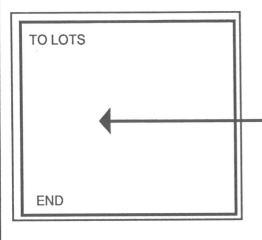

TO LOTS

END

Use your SQUARE procedure here.

© R. Sutherland   **LogoPack 1**   *Century Maths*
Stanley Thornes (Publishers) Ltd 1991

SUPERPROCEDURES

Creating your own Design

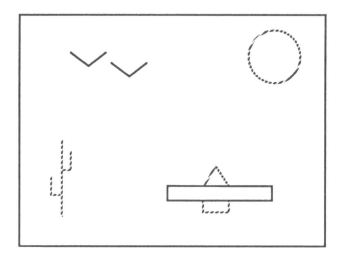

Create a picture in Logo.

Write a separate procedure for each object in the picture.

Write a separate procedure to move the turtle between objects (for example between the cactus and the sun).

Write a superprocedure to draw the whole picture.

© R. Sutherland **LogoPack 1** *Century Maths*
Stanley Thornes (Publishers) Ltd 1991

GENERAL PROCEDURES

Scaling

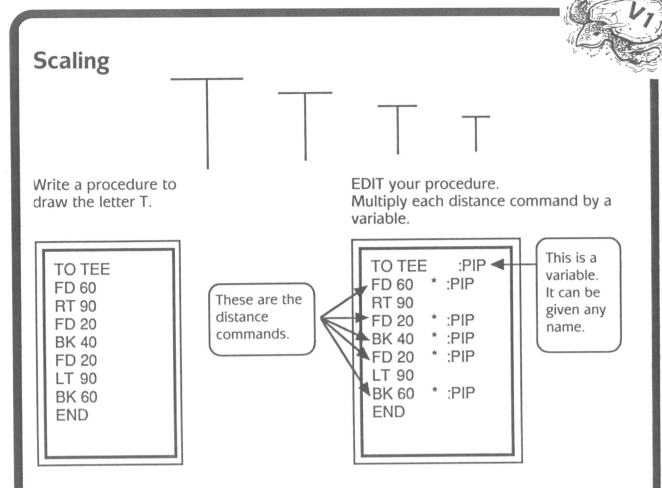

Write a procedure to
draw the letter T.

EDIT your procedure.
Multiply each distance command by a
variable.

```
TO TEE
FD 60
RT 90
FD 20
BK 40
FD 20
LT 90
BK 60
END
```

These are the
distance
commands.

```
TO TEE        :PIP
FD 60    *  :PIP
RT 90
FD 20    *  :PIP
BK 40    *  :PIP
FD 20    *  :PIP
LT 90
BK 60    *  :PIP
END
```

This is a
variable.
It can be
given any
name.

! *Don't forget to get out of the editor*
*– press Ctrl and C on the **BBC** or*
*– press Esc on the **Nimbus***

Now try TEE 1
　　　　　TEE 1.5
　　　　　TEE 0.3
　　　　　TEE − 1.3

How big can you make your T?

How small can you make your T?

Write general procedures for your own initials.

Use these procedures to make a design.

© R. Sutherland   **LogoPack 1**   *Century Maths*
Stanley Thornes (Publishers) Ltd 1991

GENERAL PROCEDURES

Operating on a Variable

20   20

60

20   20

! This line should ALWAYS be 3 times bigger than this line.

Write a procedure to draw the letter I with these measurements.

Then EDIT your EYE procedure to make it general.

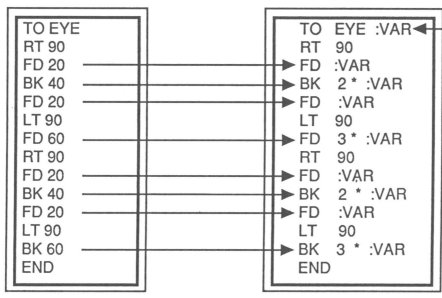

TO EYE	TO EYE :VAR
RT 90	RT 90
FD 20	FD :VAR
BK 40	BK 2 * :VAR
FD 20	FD :VAR
LT 90	LT 90
FD 60	FD 3 * :VAR
RT 90	RT 90
FD 20	FD :VAR
BK 40	BK 2 * :VAR
FD 20	FD :VAR
LT 90	LT 90
BK 60	BK 3 * :VAR
END	END

This is a variable. It can be given any name.

The 20 becomes :VAR so the 60 becomes
3 * :VAR
and the 40 becomes
2 * :VAR

! *Don't forget to get out of the editor*
– press Ctrl and C on the **BBC** <u>or</u>
– press Esc on the **Nimbus**

If you have a **BBC**, now try

EYE   20   How small can you make your I?
EYE   36
EYE   −40   How big can you make your I?

If you have a **Nimbus**, now try

EYE   5   How small can you make your I?
EYE   9
EYE   −10   How big can you make your I?

Write general procedures for your own initials.
Use these procedures to make a design.

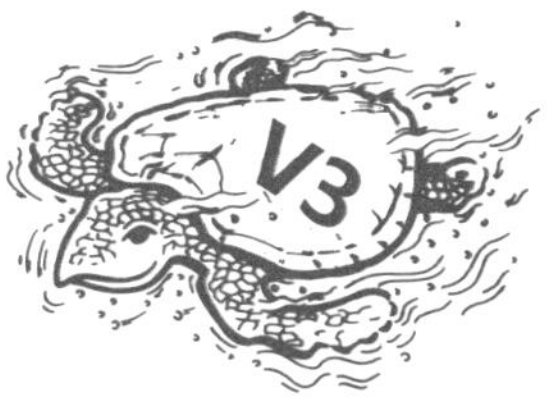

GENERAL PROCEDURES

Prediction 1

Without using the computer can you work out
what this procedure would draw if you type

PUZZLE 2

```
TO  PUZZLE   :VAR
FD 150 *  :VAR
RT 90
FD 90 *  :VAR
BK 90 *  :VAR
RT 90
FD 75 *  :VAR
LT 90
FD 65 *  :VAR
BK 65 *  :VAR
LT 90
BK 75 *  :VAR
END
```

Draw the shape for
PUZZLE 2
and label all the lengths.

What would the turtle draw if you type

PUZZLE 1.5

Draw the shape and label all the lengths.

Prediction 2

Without using the computer can you work out what this procedure would draw if you type

MYSTERY 2

```
TO MYSTERY :PIN
FD 3   * :PIN
RT 90
FD 2   * :PIN
BK 2   * :PIN
LT 90
BK 1.5 * :PIN
RT 90
FD       :PIN
BK       :PIN
LT 90
BK 1.5 * :PIN
END
```

Draw the shape for
MYSTERY 10
and label all the lengths.

What would the turtle draw if you type

MYSTERY 25

Draw the shape and label all the lengths.

© R. Sutherland **LogoPack 1** *Century Maths*
Stanley Thornes (Publishers) Ltd 1991

Choosing a Variable Name

You can choose ANY name for your variable name.

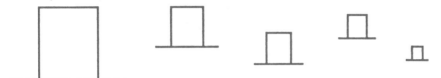

```
TO  HAT  :SILLY
RT 90
FD 3 * :SILLY
RT 90
FD 4 * :SILLY
LT 90
FD :SILLY
BK 5 * :SILLY
FD :SILLY
LT 90
FD 4 * :SILLY
END
```

Some people like to use nonsense
names like
SILLY

```
TO  HAT  :LENGTH
RT 90
FD 3 * :LENGTH
RT 90
FD 4 * :LENGTH
LT 90
FD :LENGTH
BK 5 * :LENGTH
FD :LENGTH
LT 90
FD 4 * :LENGTH
END
```

Some people like to use
meaningful names like
LENGTH

```
TO  HAT  :Y
RT 90
FD 3 * :Y
RT 90
FD 4 * :Y
LT 90
FD :Y
BK 5 * :Y
FD :Y
LT 90
FD 4 * :Y
END
```

Some people like to use single
letter names like
Y

Looks like algebra
to me

Type in the procedure HAT and change the variable name
several times. Are you convinced that the procedure is still the
same?

© R. Sutherland **LogoPack 1** *Century Maths*
Stanley Thornes (Publishers) Ltd 1991

GENERAL PROCEDURES

More than one Variable

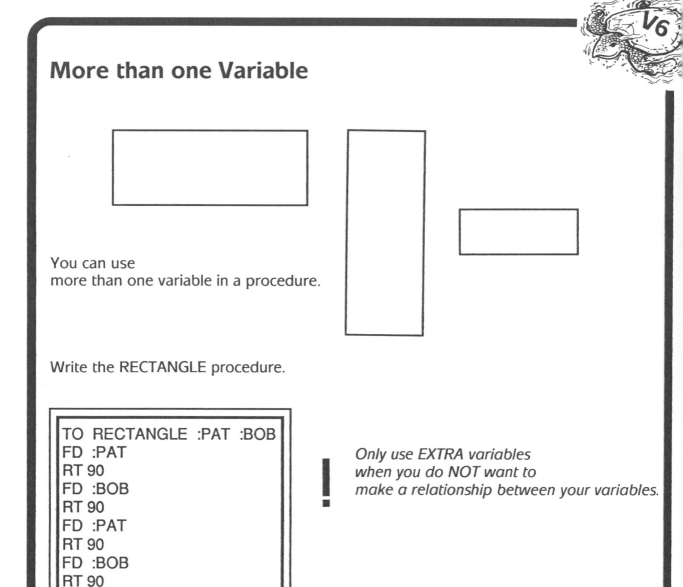

You can use
more than one variable in a procedure.

Write the RECTANGLE procedure.

```
TO  RECTANGLE  :PAT  :BOB
FD  :PAT
RT 90
FD  :BOB
RT 90
FD  :PAT
RT 90
FD  :BOB
RT 90
END
```

*Only use EXTRA variables
when you do NOT want to
make a relationship between your variables.*

Try RECTANGLE 60 120
RECTANGLE 80 40

Can you make the RECTANGLE procedure draw a square?

Make any design with the RECTANGLE procedure.

Creating your own Design

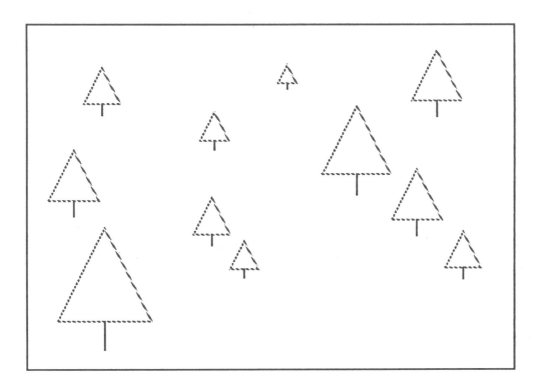

Write a general procedure to draw a tree of your own design.

Use this procedure to draw a forest of many
different sized trees – all in proportion.

A General Circle Procedure

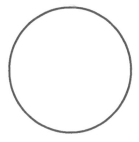

Define this procedure to draw a circle.

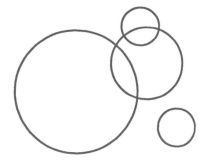

```
TO  CIRCLE
REPEAT 36 [FD 12   RT 10]
END
```

Edit CIRCLE so that it draws a bigger circle.
Change the name to BCIRCLE.

Edit CIRCLE so that it draws a smaller circle.
Change the name to SCIRCLE.

Can you write a general procedure
which will allow you to draw
different sized circles?

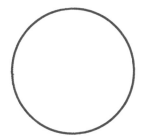

General Superprocedures

Write your own general I procedure

```
TO I :SARA



END
```

Write your own general N procedure.

```
TO N :SAM



END
```

You can use your general I procedure and your general N procedure within a new general procedure.

```
TO IN :NUM :TUM
I :NUM
N :TUM
END
```

Try: IN   3   2.5
       IN   4   6

Can you edit your IN procedure so that the I is <u>always</u> twice as big as the N?

GENERAL PROCEDURES

General Superprocedures: Prediction

Without using the computer can you work out what
the computer would draw if you type

PUZZLE 100

```
TO PUZZLE :W
SQUARE :W
MOVE :W
SQUARE :W – 10
MOVE :W – 10
SQUARE :W – 20
MOVE :W – 20
SQUARE :W – 20
END
```

```
TO SQUARE :NUM
FD :NUM
RT 90
FD :NUM
RT 90
FD :NUM
RT 90
FD :NUM
RT 90
END
```

```
TO MOVE :BIT
RT 90
PU
FD :BIT
PD
LT 90
END
```

Draw the shape for PUZZLE 100

Label all the lengths.

© R. Sutherland **LogoPack 1** *Century Maths*
Stanley Thornes (Publishers) Ltd 1991

TURTLE TURN AND ANGLE

Thinking about Angles

Make this shape by typing

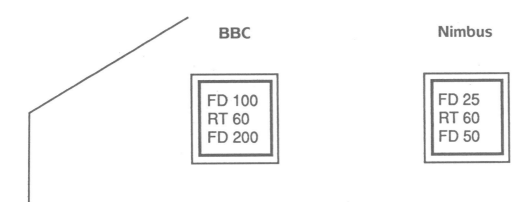

BBC

```
FD 100
RT 60
FD 200
```

Nimbus

```
FD 25
RT 60
FD 50
```

Can you change the angle and
still make the same shape?

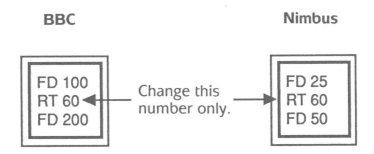

BBC

```
FD 100
RT 60
FD 200
```

Change this
number only.

Nimbus

```
FD 25
RT 60
FD 50
```

How many other angles can you use and still
make the same shape?

Measuring Angles

Design a mountain range.

Print out the design.

Label all the angles.

For example:

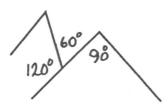

An Angle Bug

The following procedure should draw the letter N.

```
TO  NNN
FD 200
RT 135
FD 283
LT 45
FD 200
END
```

There is an angle
bug in the
procedure
and this shape is
drawn.

Can you rewrite the procedure correcting
the bug?

```
TO  NNN



END
```

TURTLE TURN AND ANGLE

Creating your own Design

Design a skyline in Logo.

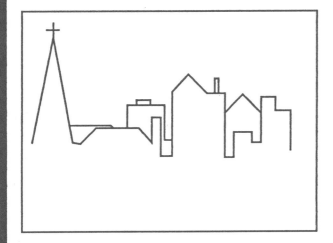

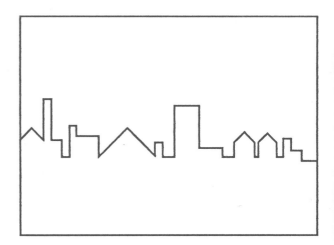

TURTLE TURN AND ANGLE

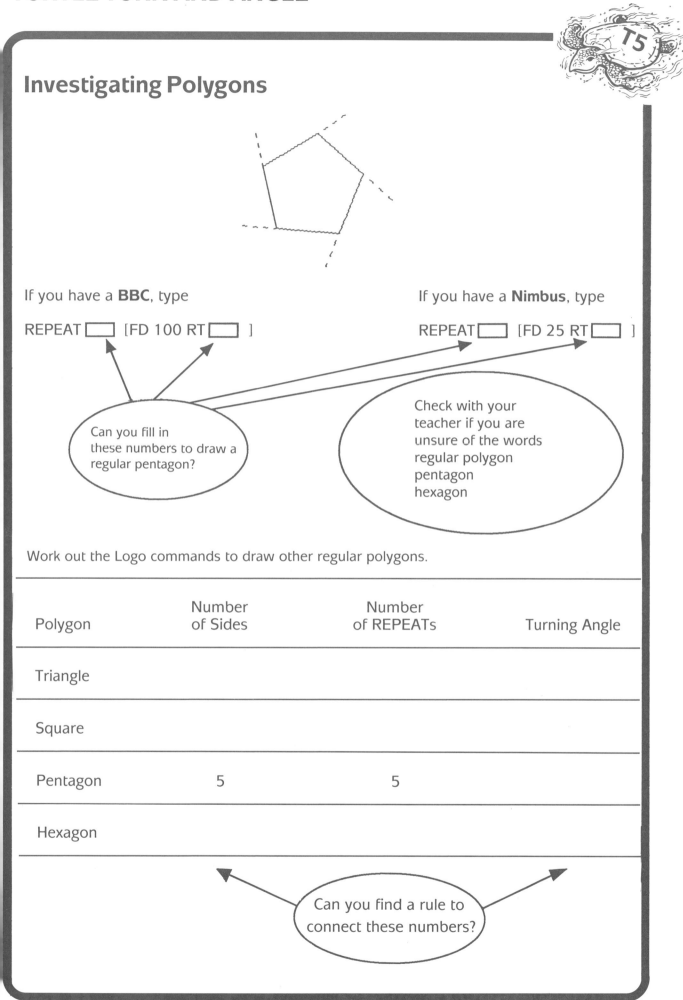

Investigating Polygons

If you have a **BBC**, type

REPEAT ☐ [FD 100 RT ☐]

If you have a **Nimbus**, type

REPEAT ☐ [FD 25 RT ☐]

Can you fill in these numbers to draw a regular pentagon?

Check with your teacher if you are unsure of the words
regular polygon
pentagon
hexagon

Work out the Logo commands to draw other regular polygons.

Polygon	Number of Sides	Number of REPEATs	Turning Angle
Triangle			
Square			
Pentagon	5	5	
Hexagon			

Can you find a rule to connect these numbers?

T5

TURTLE TURN AND ANGLE

Investigating Circles

Work out the Logo commands
to draw a circle.

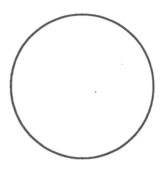

Change the commands to
draw a smaller circle.

Change the commands to
draw a larger circle.

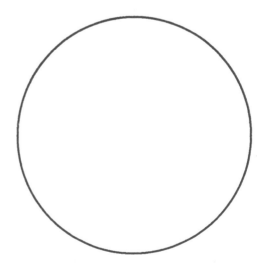

ARITHMETIC

Calculating with the Computer

You can use the computer like a calculator to do arithmetic. Try these:

> PRINT 5 + 3
>
> PRINT 9 — 6
>
> PRINT 100/5
>
> PRINT 100 * 2.5

Mental Arithmetic

Working in pairs, use the computer to give your partner some arithmetic sums.

For example, type

PRINT 10 + 13

! *Don't press the return key until your partner has worked out the answer.*

The answer is 23

PRINT 2.7 + 3.9

The answer is 6.6

Swap around when your partner has worked out the sums.

© R. Sutherland **LogoPack 1** *Century Maths*
Stanley Thornes (Publishers) Ltd 1991

ARITHMETIC

Using Decimal Numbers

Write the procedure FFF and the procedure MOVE.

| | **BBC** | **Nimbus** |
| | | |

```
TO FFF  :BIT
FD 200 *  :BIT
RT 90
FD 110 *  :BIT
BK 110 *  :BIT
RT 90
FD 80 *  :BIT
LT 90
FD 80 *  :BIT
BK 80 *  :BIT
LT 90
BK 120 *  :BIT
END
```

```
TO MOVE
RT 90
PU
FD 200
LT 90
PD
END
```

```
TO MOVE
RT 90
PU
FD 50
LT 90
PD
END
```

! *Don't forget to get out of the editor*
– press Ctrl and C on the **BBC** <u>or</u>
– press Esc on the **Nimbus**

Try FFF 1.2
     FFF 0.5
     FFF 0.7

Use the following commands to draw a row of 5 Fs which get smaller.

FFF ☐
MOVE
FFF ☐
MOVE
FFF ☐
MOVE
FFF ☐
MOVE
FFF ☐

Use these commands
and fill the decimal
inputs to FFF.

You could write a procedure
START to put the turtle in the left
hand corner of the screen.

F F F F F

© R. Sutherland **LogoPack 1** *Century Maths*
Stanley Thornes (Publishers) Ltd 1991

ARITHMETIC

Using Negative Numbers

Write the procedure T and the procedure MOVE.

BBC **Nimbus**

```
TO  T :BIT
FD 60 * :BIT
RT 90
FD 20 * :BIT
BK 40 * :BIT
FD 20 * :BIT
LT 90
BK 60 * :BIT
END
```

```
TO MOVE
RT 90
PU
FD 200
PD
LT 90
END
```

```
TO MOVE
RT 90
PU
FD 50
PD
LT 90
END
```

! *Don't forget to get out of the editor*
*– press Ctrl and C on the **BBC** <u>or</u>*
*– press Esc on the **Nimbus***

Try T − 1.5
T − 1
T − 2

Use the procedure T with negative inputs to make
a pattern of upside down Ts.

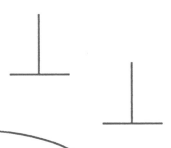

If you are not sure what
negative inputs are, check
with your teacher.

ARITHMETIC

Random Numbers

A random number is a number picked by chance.

PRINT RANDOM 10

This gives a random
number between
0 and 9.

Type this command 50
times and keep a record
of the numbers.
Do they seem random?

Can you write a Logo procedure which would give the numbers produced by
throwing a dice?

ARITHMETIC

Random Investigations

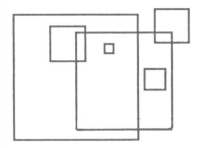

(Try PRINT RANDOM 10) The computer will print a number picked randomly from 0 to 9.

To use the RANDOM command
to draw a square of random size,
first write the procedure
SQUARE

```
TO SQUARE :SIZE
REPEAT 4 [ FD :SIZE RT 90 ]
END
```

Then, if you have a **BBC**, type:

SQUARE RANDOM 300
SQUARE RANDOM 300
SQUARE RANDOM 300

The turtle draws a square. The length of
the sides is a number picked randomly
from 0 to 299.

Then, if you have a **Nimbus**, type:

SQUARE RANDOM 75
SQUARE RANDOM 75
SQUARE RANDOM 75

The turtle draws a square. The length of
the sides is a number picked randomly
from 0 to 74.

Write this procedure:
BBC

```
TO SURPRISE
PU
SETX RANDOM 600
SETY RANDOM 300
PD
SQUARE RANDOM 300
END
```

Try changing this command to
SETX −600 + RANDOM 1200

Try REPEAT 50 [SURPRISE]

Nimbus

```
TO SURPRISE
PU
SETX RANDOM 150
SETY RANDOM 75
PD
SQUARE RANDOM 150
END
```

Try changing this command to
SETX −150 + RANDOM 300

You may want to type WINDOW
to stop the turtle wrapping
around the screen

© R. Sutherland **LogoPack 1** *Century Maths*
Stanley Thornes (Publishers) Ltd 1991

SIMILARITY AND PROPORTION

In Proportion

Write a procedure to draw any shape.

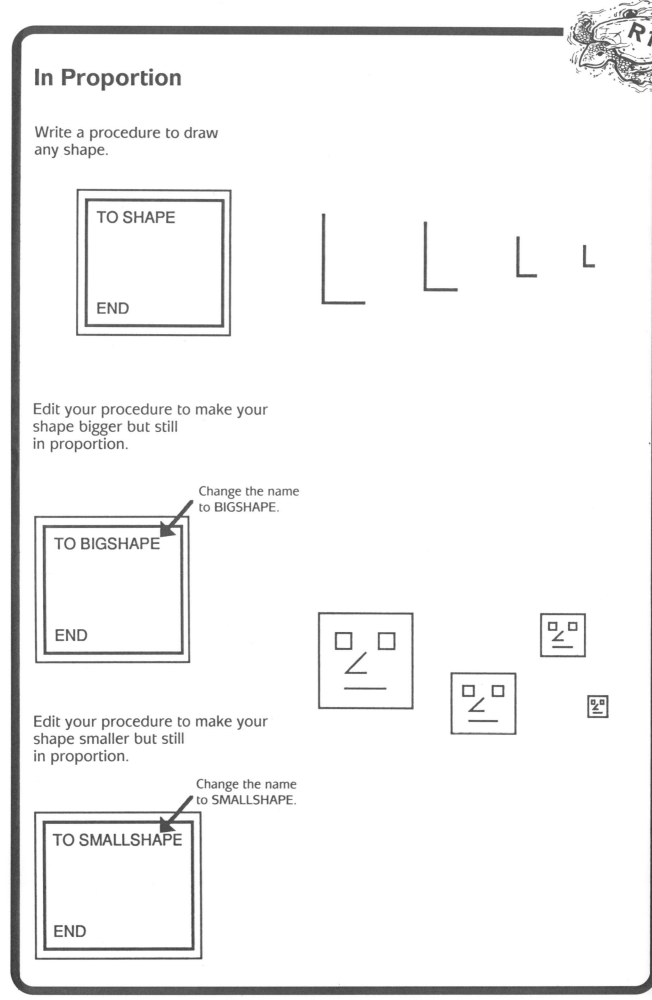

```
TO SHAPE


END
```

Edit your procedure to make your shape bigger but still in proportion.

Change the name to BIGSHAPE.

```
TO BIGSHAPE



END
```

Edit your procedure to make your shape smaller but still in proportion.

Change the name to SMALLSHAPE.

```
TO SMALLSHAPE



END
```

© R. Sutherland   **LogoPack 1**   *Century Maths*
Stanley Thornes (Publishers) Ltd 1991

Hats in Proportion

Type EDIT [HAT] to get into the editor and then define the procedure HAT.

EDIT your procedure HAT so that it will draw a hat that is bigger, but still in proportion. Change the name to BIGHAT.

EDIT your procedure HAT so that it will draw a hat that is smaller, but still in proportion. Change the name to SMALLHAT.

```
TO  HAT
RT 90
FD 60
RT 90
FD 80
LT 90
FD 20
RT 90
FD 12
RT 90
FD 100
RT 90
FD 12
RT 90
FD 20
LT 90
FD 80
END
```

```
TO  BIGHAT



END
```

```
TO  SMALLHAT



END
```

! *Don't forget to get out of the editor*
*— press Ctrl and C on the **BBC** or*
*— press Esc on the **Nimbus***

Try out HAT

Try out BIGHAT

Try out SMALLHAT

Use HAT   BIGHAT   and   SMALLHAT   to make a pattern.

© R. Sutherland **LogoPack 1** *Century Maths*
Stanley Thornes (Publishers) Ltd 1991

FUNCTIONS

Doing and Undoing

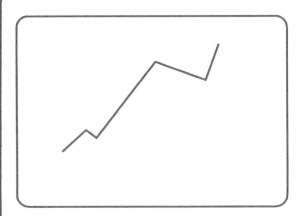

BBC

```
TO START
PU
BK 360
RT 90
BK 720
LT 90
PD
END
```

Nimbus

```
TO START
PU
BK 90
RT 90
BK 180
LT 90
PD
END
```

First write the procedure START which will put the turtle in the starting position. Then type START.

Then use FD and RT only to draw some zigzags.

Write down your commands, for example
RT 60   FD 30   RT 60   FD 70 . . .

Now hide the graphics screen by typing TS

Use the commands BK and LT to take the turtle back to the start position.

You must take the turtle back to the start without seeing the graphics screen.

Fill in the commands to draw zigzag

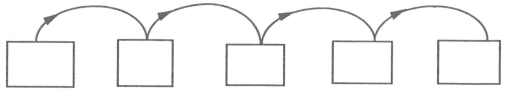

Is there a relationship between your zigzag commands and your undo zigzag commands?

Fill in the commands to undo zigzag

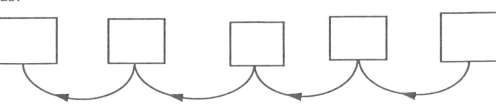

© R. Sutherland   **LogoPack 1**   *Century Maths*
Stanley Thornes (Publishers) Ltd 1991

FUNCTIONS

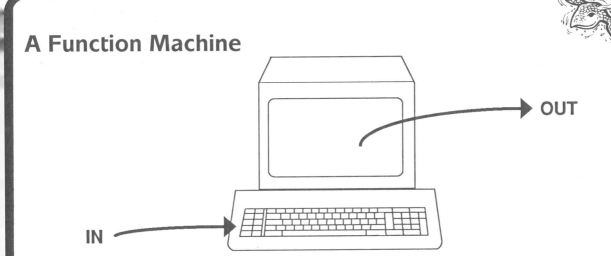

A Function Machine

You can use the computer to make a function machine.
For example, to make an ADDFOUR machine, type

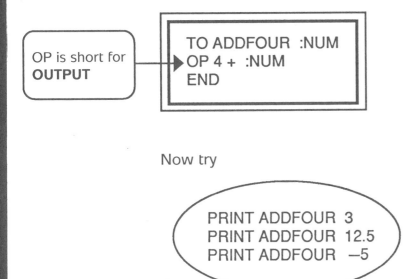

OP is short for **OUTPUT**

```
TO ADDFOUR  :NUM
OP 4 +  :NUM
END
```

Now try

PRINT ADDFOUR 3
PRINT ADDFOUR 12.5
PRINT ADDFOUR −5

Now make your own function machine.

You might like to use other operations like:

+ for addition

− for subtraction

* for multiplication

/ for division

© R. Sutherland   **LogoPack 1**   *Century Maths*
Stanley Thornes (Publishers) Ltd 1991

FUNCTIONS

Guess my Function

1. Choose a partner.

2. Build a function machine without letting your partner see the function.

3. Ask your partner to put some numbers in your function machine so that she/he can guess the function.

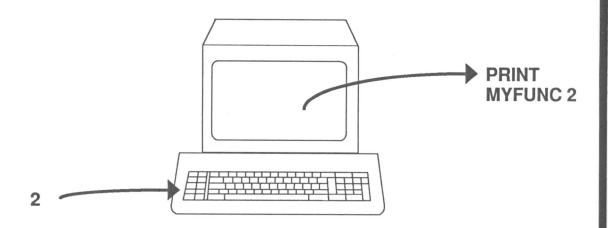

PRINT
MYFUNC 2

2

A table may help.

4. When your partner thinks she/he has guessed your function she/he must try out the idea by making a procedure for your function machine (for example, YOURFUNC).

5. Use the computer to test if YOURFUNC is the same as MYFUNC

IN	OUT
2	?
5	
1	
4	
1.5	

PRINT MYFUNC [?]

PRINT YOURFUNC [?]

FUNCTIONS

Undoing a Function

Build a function, for example:

```
TO ADDFOUR :Z
OP :Z + 4
END
```

Complete the table.
ADDFOUR FUNCTION

IN	OUT
1	
6	
5	
−4	

You can now build a function to undo the ADDFOUR function

```
TO UNDOADDFOUR :Y
OP :Y − 4
END
```

Try:

```
PRINT  UNDOADDFOUR  ADDFOUR  5
PRINT  UNDOADDFOUR  ADDFOUR  9
```

What function will undo the UNDOADDFOUR function?

Build the MULTEN function

```
TO MULTEN :X
OP :X * 10
END
```

Can you build the UNDOMULTEN function?
(You might want to call it a shorter name.)

Build the SUBFIVE function

```
TO SUBFIVE :Z
OP :Z − 5
END
```

Can you build the UNDOSUBFIVE function?

© R. Sutherland   **LogoPack 1**   *Century Maths*
Stanley Thornes (Publishers) Ltd 1991

FUNCTIONS

Fun with Functions

Build two function machines; for example

```
TO ADDFOUR :X
OP :X + 4
END
```

```
TO MULTEN :Y
OP :Y * 10
END
```

What happens when you type:

PRINT   ADDFOUR   MULTEN 5

Use some other numbers to try out the function machines.

Try to complete the table without using the computer and then check your results.

ADDFOUR   MULTEN   MACHINE

IN	OUT
1	
2	
5	
9	
-7	
-3	

Is ADDFOUR MULTEN 3

the same as

MULTEN ADDFOUR 3

Give a reason for your answer.

FUNCTIONS

Algebra Expressions – 1

Write procedures for the following two functions:

```
TO FUNA :Y
OP 2 * (:Y + 5)
END
```

```
TO FUNB :Y
OP 2 * :Y + 10
END
```

Don't forget to get out of the editor
*– press Ctrl and C on the **BBC** <u>or</u>*
*– press Esc on the **Nimbus***

Try PRINT FUNA 3

Try PRINT FUNB 10

Fill in the following table

Fill in the following table

FUNA

IN	OUT
− 150	
− 20.5	
0	
3	16
5.9	

FUNB

IN	OUT
− 150	
− 20.5	
0	10
3	
5.9	

Are FUNA and FUNB the same?

Write down a reason for your answer.

FUNCTIONS

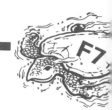

Algebra Expressions – 2

Write procedures for the following two functions:

```
TO FUNA  :W
OP 7 * (5 – :W)
END
```

```
TO FUNB  :W
OP 35 – :W
END
```

 Don't forget to get out of the editor
– press Ctrl and C on the **BBC** *or*
– press Esc on the **Nimbus**

Try PRINT FUNA 0

Try PRINT FUNB 0

Fill in the following table

Fill in the following table

FUNA

IN	OUT
– 150	
– 10	
0	35
17.5	
36	

FUNB

IN	OUT
– 150	
– 10	
0	35
17.5	
36	

Are FUNA and FUNB the same?

Write down a reason for your answer.

© R. Sutherland **LogoPack 1** *Century Maths*
Stanley Thornes (Publishers) Ltd 1991

FUNCTIONS

A Function Investigation

Write procedures for the following two functions:

```
TO FUNNY  :X
OP 5 +  :X
END
```

```
TO SUNNY  :Y
OP 5 *  :Y
END
```

Try PRINT FUNNY 3 and PRINT SUNNY 3

FUNNY

IN	OUT
−3 ⟶	
−1 ⟶	
0 ⟶	
0.2 ⟶	
0.5 ⟶	
0.8 ⟶	
1 ⟶	
3 ⟶	
7 ⟶	

SUNNY

IN	OUT
−3 ⟶	
−1 ⟶	
0 ⟶	
0.2 ⟶	
0.5 ⟶	
0.8 ⟶	
1 ⟶	
3 ⟶	
7 ⟶	

Try some more numbers and fill in the two tables.

When does FUNNY output a larger number than SUNNY?

When does FUNNY output a smaller number than SUNNY?

When do FUNNY and SUNNY output the same number?

© R. Sutherland **LogoPack 1** *Century Maths*
Stanley Thornes (Publishers) Ltd 1991

FUNCTIONS

A Puzzle

Syreeta says:

> I multiply an unknown number by 5 and then add 12.
>
> I subtract the unknown number and divide the result by 4.
>
> It seems that I always get 3 more than the number I started with.
>
> I think that would happen whatever number I start with.

Can you write a Logo
procedure to show
that Syreeta is right?

COORDINATES AND TURTLE HEADING

Coordinates and the Hidden Grid

BBC

This procedure will draw axes (grid lines).

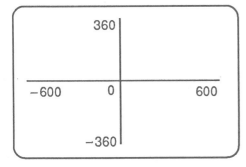

```
TO AXES
CS
FD 360
BK 720
FD 360
RT 90
FD 600
BK 1200
FD 600
LT 90
END
```

NIMBUS

This procedure will draw axes (grid lines).

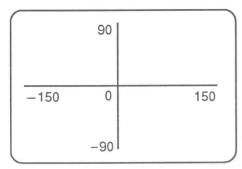

```
TO AXES
CS
FD 90
BK 180
FD 90
RT 90
FD 150
BK 300
FD 150
LT 90
END
```

On your screen there is a hidden grid.

You can use coordinate commands to place the turtle on this grid.

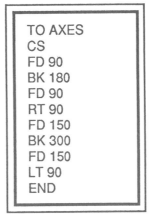

If you are not sure what coordinates are, check with your teacher.

Try the following coordinate commands:

```
SETX      50
SETX    −150
SETY    −100
SETPOS  [ −100  80]
```

Other useful commands:
XCOR
YCOR
POS

Use the coordinates to put the turtle in a new position, and then draw a picture.

Wallpaper Designs

Write a procedure to draw a flower.

TO FLOWER

END

Make the turtle return to the same position and face in the same direction at the end of the procedure.

Use this FLOWER procedure to make a wallpaper design.

COORDINATES AND TURTLE HEADING

Tile Designs

Design a tile with the turtle.

Make the turtle return to the same position, facing in the same direction at the end of your tile design.

Write a procedure for your tile design.

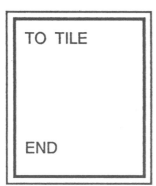

Use this TILE procedure to produce a pattern of tiles.

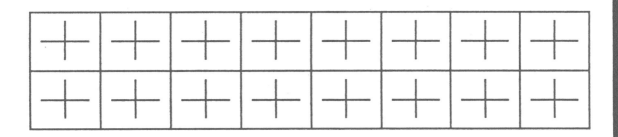

Turtle Heading

You can use SETH to change the turtle's heading. Try this:

```
SETH 45
FD 80
SETH 160
FD 80
SETH —250
FD 100
```

Use SETH to draw a compass.

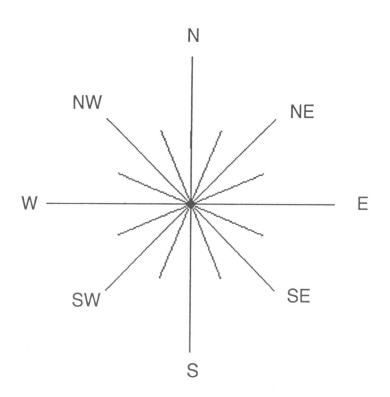

Other useful commands:

HEADING

GRAPHS

Coordinates and Graphs

Write the AXES procedure and the SPOT procedure.

Nimbus

```
TO AXES
CS
FD 90
BK 180
FD 90
RT 90
FD 150
BK 300
FD 150
LT 90
END
```

BBC

```
TO AXES
CS
FD 360
BK 720
FD 360
RT 90
FD 600
BK 1200
FD 600
LT 90
END
```

```
TO SPOT  :A  :B
PU
HT
SETX  :A
SETY  :B
PD
FD 0
END
```

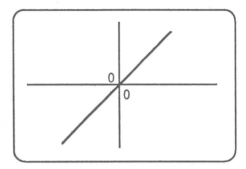

Type:

WINDOW
AXES

BBC

SPOT 0 0	Continue to use SPOT with different inputs
SPOT 100 200	until a straight line is drawn across
SPOT − 80 − 160	the screen.
SPOT 50 100	If you make a mistake type AXES and
SPOT − 70 − 140	start again.

Nimbus

SPOT 0 0	Continue to use SPOT with different inputs
SPOT 25 50	until a straight line is drawn across
SPOT − 20 − 40	the screen.
SPOT 50 100	If you make a mistake type AXES and
SPOT − 70 − 140	start again.

Fill in this table with your new coordinates

This is the graph of
$y = 2x$

100	200

Can you draw a collection of straight
lines all parallel to one another?

© R. Sutherland **LogoPack 1** *Century Maths*
Stanley Thornes (Publishers) Ltd 1991

GRAPHS

Straight Line Graphs

This procedure will draw axes.

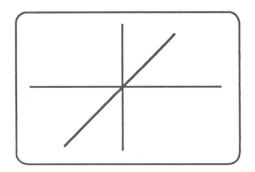

BBC

```
TO AXES
CS
FD 360
BK 720
FD 360
RT 90
FD 600
BK 1200
FD 600
LT 90
END
```

Nimbus

```
TO AXES
CS
FD 90
BK 180
FD 90
RT 90
FD 150
BK 300
FD 150
LT 90
END
```

You can draw this graph by plotting all the points
separately or you can write a Logo procedure
to do it more quickly.

Type in the procedure LINE1

BBC

```
TO LINE1  :X
IF XCOR> 300 [STOP]
HT
SETPOS  SE :X 2 * :X
LINE1  :X + 10
END
```

Nimbus

```
TO LINE1  :X
IF XCOR> 75 [STOP]
HT
SETPOS  SE :X 2 * :X
FD 0
LINE1  :X + 0.5
END
```

In mathematics this graph is
called $y = 2x$
because the y value is always
twice as big as the x value.

Try LINE1 −150

Try LINE1 −75

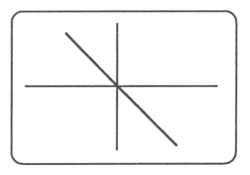

Can you change the
procedure LINE1 to
draw a graph which
looks like...

What is the
name of
this graph?

GEOMETRIC TRANSFORMATIONS

Reflection

Write the procedure PAT to draw this shape.

EDIT the procedure PAT so that the new procedure draws the reflection of PAT. Only change the turtle turn commands.

```
TO PAT
RT 30
FD 100
RT 100
FD 40
END
```

```
TO REPAT


END
```

Can you edit PAT to produce all of these reflections?

Useful commands:

SETPOS [0 0]
PU
PD

GEOMETRIC TRANSFORMATIONS

Symmetrical Patterns

Write a Logo procedure to draw the right half of a butterfly.

```
TO RIGHTBFLY



END
```

Edit your procedure so that it will draw the reflection of RIGHTBFLY.
Change the name to LEFTBFLY.

Put RIGHTBFLY and LEFTBFLY together in a BUTTERFLY procedure.

```
TO BUTTERFLY    ←
END
```

Use RIGHTBFLY
and LEFTBFFLY
in your BUTTERFLY
procedure

Use BUTTERFLY to make a picture of butterflies.

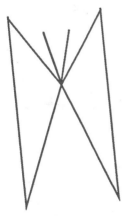

GEOMETRIC TRANSFORMATIONS

Rotation

Write a Logo procedure to draw a person.

```
TO PERSON


END
```

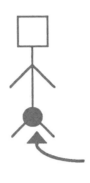

Make the turtle
start and finish
at the same place,
pointing in the
same direction.

Use this procedure to rotate the
person about a point.

Change this procedure to produce another pattern.

© R. Sutherland   **LogoPack 1**   *Century Maths*
Stanley Thornes (Publishers) Ltd 1991

Spirals

Type this SPIRAL procedure into the computer.

```
TO SPIRAL  :LEN
FD  :LEN
RT 90
SPIRAL  :LEN + 5
END
```

This is called a
recursive procedure
because it makes a
copy of itself.

! Don't forget to get out of the editor
 – press Ctrl and C on the **BBC** <u>or</u>
 – press Esc on the **Nimbus**

You can press the
ESC key to stop the
procedure.

Now type SPIRAL 10

```
TO SPIRAL  :LEN
IF  :LEN > 200 [STOP]
FD  :LEN
RT 90
SPIRAL  :LEN + 5
END
```

Try putting this
conditional command
into your procedure.

Now type SPIRAL 10

A conditional command is
one which will either do
something or not do
something depending on
a condition which you decide.

Change the recursive line
SPIRAL :LEN + 5 to
SPIRAL :LEN − 5
 – you will also need to
change the conditional
command.

SPIRALS/RECURSION

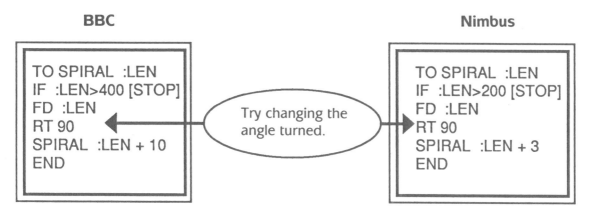

Investigating spirals

Type this SPIRAL procedure into the computer.

BBC

```
TO SPIRAL  :LEN
IF  :LEN>400 [STOP]
FD  :LEN
RT 90
SPIRAL  :LEN + 10
END
```

Try changing the angle turned.

Nimbus

```
TO SPIRAL  :LEN
IF  :LEN>200 [STOP]
FD  :LEN
RT 90
SPIRAL  :LEN + 3
END
```

! *Don't forget to get out of the editor*
 ■ *– press Ctrl and C on the **BBC** <u>or</u>*
 *– press Esc on the **Nimbus***

Type SPIRAL 10

EDIT the procedure by changing the turning angle to
RT 87

Get out of the editor and type
SPIRAL 10

Investigate the links between
the angle turned and the
'rays' of the spiral.

Put your results into a table.

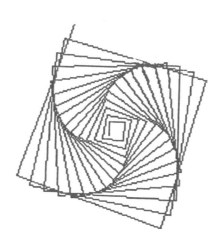

This one has 4 rays.

Turtle turn	Number of 'rays'
92	4

Spiral Sequences

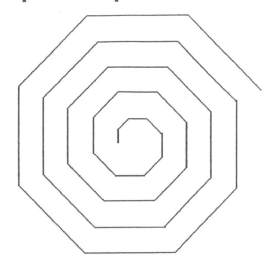

10   20   30   40   50 . . .

Type in the following procedures:

BBC

```
TO SPISEQ :NUM
IF :NUM > 250 [STOP]
FD :NUM
RT 45
TYPE :NUM
TYPE CHAR 32
SPISEQ :NUM +10
END
```

◄— This types a space —►

Nimbus

```
TO SPISEQ :NUM
IF :NUM > 250 [STOP]
FD :NUM
RT 45
TYPE :NUM
TYPE [\20]
SPISEQ :NUM +10
END
```

Now try SPISEQ 10

Try out some other spirals sequences, for example

5   10   15   20   25   30   35 . . .

10   15   22.5   33.75 . . .

TEACHER'S GUIDE

Contents

Introduction and aims

The aim of the activities in LogoPack 1 is to introduce pupils both to important aspects of the Logo[1] language and a range of mathematical ideas. These two aims are often very closely linked, so for example the idea of variable in Logo is closely related to a number of algebraic ideas. Similarly the idea of turtle turn is closely related to the idea of angle. Pupils can work in the Logo environment without making links with their other mathematical work and as a teacher you will have an important role in pointing out the similarities and differences between the two environments.

The pack includes:

- a Teacher's Guide
- a LogoPack Map
- a set of Pupils' Worksheets
- a Glossary of Logo Commands

The pupil worksheets are not intended to be used in a linear sequence. There is, however, a partial ordering within the materials which is represented in the LogoPack Map and discussed in *Organisation of the LogoPack*. The LogoPack Map is designed to be displayed as a poster on the classroom wall, to be used by both pupils and teacher. The Glossary of Commands is mainly for reference and lists all the commands used in the pack, with a brief explanation on each command.

The Logo and mathematics ideas presented in the pack are appropriate for Key Stage 3 and do not represent the whole potential of Logo as a programming language. Similarly this teacher's guide is only meant to provide an overview of the language and for more comprehensive information we suggest you read the Logo guide which accompanies your school software. The best way to become more confident with Logo is to find a computer and start trying some of the activities in the LogoPack. More Logo-mathematics ideas can be found in the publications described in the bibliography.

Computer work in the mathematics classroom is only of value if pupils reflect on the mathematical ideas being used, and make decisions and solve problems for themselves. The way you as a teacher first introduce the Logo activity is critical and pupils must develop confidence in their own problem solving ability. We have found a number of factors which increase motivation and level of engagement in the Logo activity which are:

- pupils working in pairs and discussing
- teacher intervention which encourages reflection
- pupils working on their own projects
- pupils keeping a written record of their work
- pupils being actively encouraged to debug their mistakes

---

[1]The Logo materials are suitable for Nimbus Logo (version 2.0J), and Logotron Logo for the BBC and the Archimedes computer.

Although some of the Logo activities in the pack are relatively well-defined they all allow for the possibility of open ended extension and this should be encouraged.

In carrying out the Logo tasks within this pack pupils will begin to use and understand a range of mathematical ideas which includes angle, number, algebra, ratio and proportion, coordinates, functions and graphs, reflections and rotation. Table 1 presents a list of all the activities in the pack, with an overview of the mathematical and programming ideas which pupils are likely to use when carrying out the activity. Which ideas pupils do use depends, to a certain extent, on what you as a teacher choose to emphasise when you introduce the activity.

Particular aspects of the computer environment will vary depending on the type of computer you are using and on whether or not it is a network or stand alone system. Hopefully you will be able to find out the details of your own computer setup from the documentation which comes with your school computers and from other members of staff. You will probably experience some frustration when you first attempt to get Logo running on your school system, but once this hurdle is over the use of Logo in the classroom will become reasonably straightforward.

The Logo language

Background

The Logo syntax is completely precise and exploration in Logo does not mean discovering the syntax for yourself. Pupils need to know the syntax and the structure of the language and this is why certain activities are well defined.

Logo was developed from the language LISP – a language for computer science and Artificial Intelligence (see Papert's *Mindstorms* for a discussion of the philosophy surrounding Logo). As with all programming languages it has certain characteristics which you and your pupils will need to become familiar with. Firstly it comes with a set of Logo commands (or primitives) which the computer understands when Logo is loaded. You can add new commands to the language, which is why Logo is called an extensible language. Logo is best known for the turtle graphics subset of the language. Here the programmer controls either a floor turtle or a screen turtle (which usually looks like a triangle). As Papert says, 'The turtle serves no other purpose other than of being good to program with and good to think with.'

Interacting with the computer

When you work in Logo the computer screen looks different depending on whether or not you are interacting with the *text* screen, the *graphics* screen or the *edit* screen. When you first load into Logo[2] you will interact with the text screen. Here the screen is completely taken over by the text code, good for calculations, but not good for doing graphics. When you type CS (for clearscreen) the screen will change to being predominantly a graphics screen, with a small amount of text screen underneath (Figure 1).

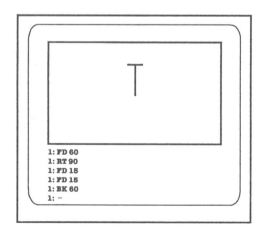

Figure 1   Graphics screen

---

[2]This description relates to RML Logo for the BBC computer. Other systems may be slightly different.

If you now enter some turtle graphics commands, for example:

FD 120
RT 90
FD 30
BK 60

the turtle will draw the letter T which is shown in Figure 1. You are interacting directly with the graphics output and each Logo graphics command produces an effect on the screen. In this interactive mode the Logo commands are not remembered after they have been typed into the computer.

Writing a procedure

If you want to keep a computer record of the commands which have drawn your Logo picture you must write a procedure. A procedure is a group of commands which have been given a name. It is the procedural nature of Logo which encourages the user to break a problem into simpler component parts. Defining procedures is like adding new Logo commands to the language, and procedures can be saved on a disk to be used whenever they are needed again.

In order to define a procedure you firstly choose a name for your group of commands (for example, TEE) and then you type EDIT [TEE].[3] At this point the screen changes to the EDIT screen (Figure 2).

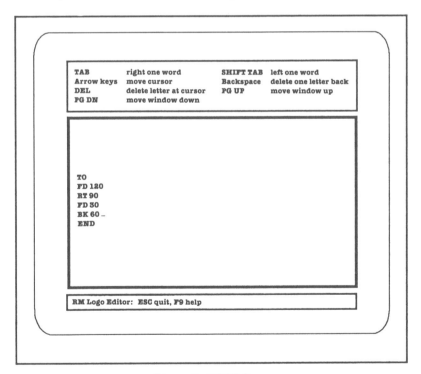

Figure 2   EDIT Screen

---

[3]It is also possible to define a procedure by typing TO TEE. We have chosen to use EDIT [TEE] because we think that this helps pupils to understand the importance of the editor.

When you are in the editor you type in the commands for your procedure, pressing Ctrl and C (or Esc on the Nimbus machine) to get out of the editor and define your procedure. If, when you are out of the editor, you type:

TEE

the screen will change to the graphics screen and the letter T will be drawn.

It is a good idea if pupils' first procedure is to draw a relatively simple shape using commands which have already been tried out by interacting directly with the computer. Some pupils may want to define procedures directly in the editor without reflecting on the processes involved and this should be discouraged.

Although at the moment we are talking about procedures for drawing pictures the idea of a procedure (i.e. a set of commands) is the same for other aspects of Logo (for example, for doing an arithmetic calculation).

Editing a procedure

You may, for some reason, not be satisfied with your procedure. There may be a mistake in your commands or you may want to modify or extend what you have written. In the example of the letter T the turtle does not start and end in the same place on the screen. This could be a nuisance, if for example you wanted to draw a row of Ts. So to edit your procedure to make the turtle start and end in the same place you first type:

EDIT [TEE]

This takes you back into the editor again. When you are in the editor you can use the arrow and the delete keys to insert and delete lines. In this example if you insert the commands

FD 30
LT 90
BK 120

at the end of the procedure it will produce the desired effect.

In this pack considerable emphasis is placed on the idea of writing and editing a procedure and many other ideas depend on pupils confidently being able to do this. They need to know that if they make a mistake in their procedure they can correct it using the editor and they need to be confident at getting in and out of the editor.

Aids to debugging

If you make a mistake in your procedure it is often very difficult to find out where this mistake occurs. One very helpful command is WALK. If you type

WALK [TEE]

the computer has now been instructed to execute the procedure TEE line by line and will only carry out the Logo command after the return key has been pressed. Using WALK with a procedure helps pupils to understand the way in which Logo carries out the commands in a step by step manner. To stop the WALKing process you use the command UNWALK.

Superprocedures

Procedures can be collected together into **superprocedures** (see Figure 3).
Pupils often find this idea useful as their goal evolves (see for example the
activity *Superprocedures: Building Up*). Alternatively they may break down
their problem into parts (see for example the activity *Superprocedures:
Breaking Down*). Analysing a problem into parts does not seem to be
straightforward for most pupils and so as a teacher you will need to
emphasise this idea when you consider it to be an important problem
solving strategy.

```
TO OCT
REPEAT 8 [FD 30 LT 45]
END
```

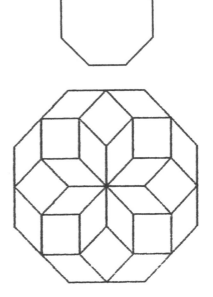

```
TO OCTHOUSE
REPEAT 8 [OCT]
END
```

Figure 3   The superprocedure (OCTHOUSE)

You may also want to emphasise the idea of writing a procedure for the
navigating commands (i.e. the commands which take you from one picture
to another) which is separate from the procedure for the picture commands,
as has been done in the procedure ROW in Figure 4.

```
TO ROW          TO START         TO MOVE
START           PU               PU
TEE 15          LT 90            RT 90
MOVE            FD 80            FD 40
TEE 10          RT 90            LT 90
MOVE            PD               PD
TEE 5           END              END
END
```

Figure 4   Procedure for a row of Ts

Saving pupils' work

Pupils need to be able to save and retrieve their procedures from previous sessions. If they cannot do this they are unlikely to realise the potential of defining procedures as reusable modules. They also need to understand that when they use the SAVE command in Logo all the procedures in the working memory are saved in the named file (i.e. you do not have to save each procedure separately). This is why it is important that the name of their file for storing their procedures on disk is not the same as the name of any of their procedures.

After some time pupils may have saved too many procedures within their file and they should learn how to erase procedures from the working memory before saving to their file (using ERASE).

General procedures

Until now we have been talking about procedures which will draw a shape in one size only. In Logo it is possible to write a **general procedure**, that is a procedure which will draw a shape in any size which you choose (or produce a general algorithm). In order to do this you use the idea of variable input. One way of making the TEE procedure a general procedure is shown in Figure 5.

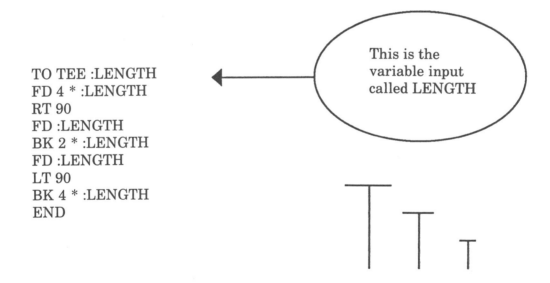

```
TO TEE :LENGTH
FD 4 * :LENGTH
RT 90
FD :LENGTH
BK 2 * :LENGTH
FD :LENGTH
LT 90
BK 4 * :LENGTH
END
```

This is the variable input called LENGTH

Figure 5   A general procedure

We have chosen the name :LENGTH for the variable name but it is possible to use any name, including nonsense names and single letter names. It is important that pupils realise that the computer does not understand the name itself, and the name represents a variable input. For this reason we often encourage pupils to use 'nonsense' names and they themselves often choose to use single letter names, because this involves less typing. Too much emphasis on the computer science idea of 'meaningful variable names' conflicts with the algebraically important idea that the name itself is arbitrary (for example $f(a)=5a$ is mathematically equivalent to $f(b)=5b$).

Within these materials we have stressed the idea of operating on a variable in a general procedure instead of the idea of producing new additional unrelated variables. This is because we believe that making a mathematical relationship explicit is important for pupils' developing algebraic understanding. As long as the relationships are initially straightforward (for example multiples of 5) pupils can begin to use the idea of operating on a variable within a number of Logo situations. The general procedure HAT (Figure 6) was written by two eleven-year pupils after six hours of Logo programming.

```
TO HAT :DEBBIE
FD 10 * :DEBBIE
RT 90
FD 3 * :DEBBIE
RT 90
FD 10 * :DEBBIE
LT 90
FD 3 * :DEBBIE
RT 90
FD :DEBBIE
RT 90
FD 9 * :DEBBIE
RT 90
FD :DEBBIE
RT 90
FD 3 * :DEBBIE
END
```

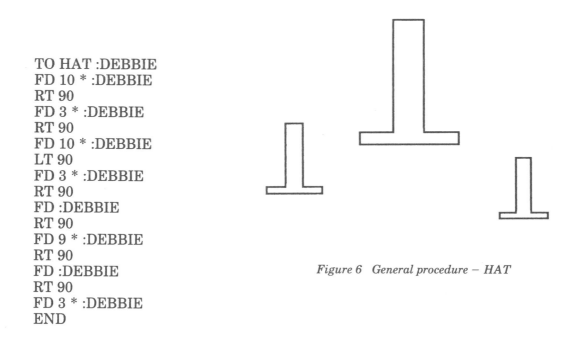

Figure 6   General procedure – HAT

We have also introduced the idea of variable input as a scale factor (see the activity *General Procedures: Scaling*) because this is another mathematically important way for pupils to construct a general procedure.

Within the pack we have emphasised the idea of pupils constructing their own procedures, as opposed to reading other people's procedures. But we have included a number of prediction tasks (see for example the activity *General Procedures: Prediction 1*) which encourage pupils to think about the effects of a general procedure when specific values are input into the procedure. Asking pupils to predict the effects of procedures written by other pupils could become a valuable part of classroom discussion and activity.

Two of the LogoPack activities (V9 and V10) are concerned with writing general superprocedures which use a general procedure. This idea often arises naturally as pupils decide to use their general Logo procedure within a more extended project.

Functions in Logo

Functions are procedures which output values to be used by other commands or procedures. So for example if you want to write a Logo procedure which will calculate the square of any number you could write

```
TO SQUARE :NUM
OP :NUM * :NUM
END
```

If you then type:

```
FD SQUARE 9
```

the computer would firstly calculate the square of 9 and then output this value (81) to be used as input to the FD command. The result is that the turtle would move forward 81 steps.

Logo functions behave in a similar way to mathematical functions, so if you define a procedure:

```
TO F :y            equivalent to F(y) = y + 5
OP :y + 5
END
```

and

```
TO G :y            equivalent to G(y) = 3y
OP 3 * :y
END
```

you can then define the composite function

```
TO H :y            equivalent to H(y) = F(G(y))
OP F G :y
END
```

The idea of a composite function is introduced in the activity *Fun With Functions*. Composite functions are a useful idea in Logo and provide an important basis for subsequent work with mathematical functions.

Recursion

Recursion can be used whenever you want to reproduce a nested set of increasing or decreasing geometrical images. In this pack the idea of recursion is introduced through the task of drawing a spiral (see the activity *Spirals*). The spiral procedure is a tail recursive procedure because the recursive call is the last line of the procedure (Figure 7a). Unexpected results occur for full recursion, when the recursive call is no longer the last line (see Figure 7b).

Recursion is a very powerful programming structure which is dealt with in detail in LogoPack 2. When pupils start to experiment with recursive procedures it is valuable for them to use the WALK facility, because this will help develop a model of the way the computer processes a recursive procedure.

```
TO SPIRAL :LEN
IF :LEN > 50 [STOP]
FD :LEN
RT 90
SPIRAL :LEN + 5
END
```

```
TO UNEXPECTED :LEN
IF :LEN > 50 [STOP]
FD :LEN
RT 90
UNEXPECTED :LEN + 5
FD :LEN
LT 90
END
```

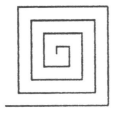

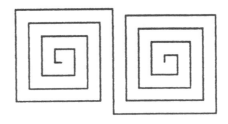

Figure 7a   Tail recursive procedure   *Figure 7b   Full recursive procedure*

Coordinates and graph plotting

The value of Logo turtle graphics commands (for example, FD and RT) is that they are local commands, each movement of the turtle is relative to the previous movement. Giving turtle graphics commands to the turtle is like giving commands to your own body. Sometimes, however, it is useful to use *x,y* coordinate commands, which are global in nature. If, for example, you are producing a wallpaper pattern on the screen you may want to use the coordinate commands to put the turtle in the correct place to begin each row of the wallpaper design. Coordinate commands should be used with caution because they destroy the modular nature of a Logo procedure. For example if you use SETX 50 in a procedure you can no longer place your procedure in any position on the screen.

Global coordinates are also important for graph plotting in Logo. The LogoPack introduces pupils to the idea of plotting graphs in Logo. Some pupils may want to develop their own more efficient graph plotting microworld, whereas for others it might be more appropriate for them to be introduced to LogoPlotter, or another graph plotting environment.

Organisation of the LogoPack

The LogoPack Map presents an overview of the organisational structure of the LogoPack. Activities have sometimes been grouped together with a Logo focus (for example, Beginning Logo Commands) and other times with a more mathematical focus (for example, Functions) but in all cases both Logo and mathematical ideas are intermingled. The two central Logo ideas within the pack are the idea of a procedure and the idea of a general procedure and two of the blocks focus on these ideas. It is much more important to make sure that your pupils are confident with these ideas than it is to rush through all the worksheets in the pack.

If possible, pupils should work on a more extended Logo project (for example, *Earring Designs*) at the same time as they are working on a more prescriptive task (for example, *General Procedures: Scaling*). Project ideas are presented within many of the blocks, but there are many project ideas within the *Century Maths* Theme books.

Table 1 lists all the worksheets in the pack suggesting the **mathematical ideas** which pupils are likely to use when working on a particular activity. It is important to realise that pupils will not necessarily use these ideas, as there will be many perfectly acceptable ways of solving a problem which cannot be predicted in advance. The mathematical ideas which pupils use will reflect the mathematics culture in your own classroom. We have not included problem solving ideas (for example, breaking a problem into parts) in this table because they are too complex to classify in this type of table.

Logo Pack Map

Other Logo Commands
Useful pen and screen
commands (O1)

Other Logo Commands
The REPEAT command (O2)

Functions
Doing and undoing (F1)
Function machines (F2, F3)
Undoing a function (F4)
Fun with functions (F5)
Algebra expressions (F6, F7)
A function investigation (F8)
A puzzle (F9)

Coordinates and Turtle Heading
Coordinates and the hidden grid (C1)
Wallpaper designs (C2)
Tile designs (C3)
Turtle heading (C4)

Graphs
Coordinates and graphs (G1)
Straight line graphs (G2)

Beginning Logo Commands
Turtle geometry 1: FD and BK: RT and LT (B1)
Turtle Geometry 2: CLEAN, CS: ST and HT: PU and PD: PE (B2)
Logo people (B3)
Logo challenge (B4)

Arithmetic
Calculating with
the computer (A1)

General Procedures
Scaling (V1)
Operating on a variable (V2)
Predicting tasks (V3, V4)
Choosing a variable name (V5)
More than one variable (V6)
Creating your own designs (V7)
A general circle procedure (V8)

Similarity and Proportion
In proportion (R1)
Hats in proportion (R2)

More Arithmetic
Using decimal numbers (A2)
Using negative numbers (A3)
Random numbers (A4)
Random investigations (A5)

Geometric Transformations
Reflection (TR1)
Symmetrical patterns (TR2)
Rotation (TR3)

Turtle Turn and Angle
Thinking about angles (T1)
Measuring angles (T2)
An angle bug (T3)
Creating your own design (T4)
Investigating polygons (T5)
Investigating circles (T6)

Procedures
Defining and editing a procedure (P1)
Moving procedures about (P2)
Saving and loading procedures (P3)
Earring designs (P4)
Movement (p5)

Superprocedures
Building up (S1)
Breaking down (S2)
Creating your own design (S3)

General Superprocedures
V9, V10

Spirals/Recursion
Spirals (RR1)
Investigating spirals (RR2)
Spiral sequences (RR3)

Table 1 – Mathematical Ideas

	Length	Estimation	Angle	Direction	Decimals	Negative numbers	Scale	Algebra	Geometric transformations	Ratio and proportion	Coordinates	Graphs	Random processes
(B) Beginning Logo Commands													
(B1) Turtle Geometry 1	✓	✓	✓										
(B2) Turtle Geometry 2	✓	✓	✓										
(B3) Logo People	✓	✓	✓										
(B4) Logo Challenge	✓	✓	✓										
(P) Procedures													
(P1) Defining and Editing a Procedure	✓	✓	✓										
(P2) Moving Procedures About													
(P3) Saving and Loading Procedures													
(P4) Earring Designs	✓	✓	✓										
(P5) Movement	✓	✓	✓										
(O) Other Logo Commands													
(O1) Useful Pen and Screen Commands													
(O2) The REPEAT Command													
(S) Superprocedures													
(S1) Building Up	✓	✓	✓										
(S2) Breaking Down	✓	✓	✓										
(S3) Creating your own Design	✓	✓	✓										
(V) General Procedures													
(V1) Scaling	✓	✓			✓	✓	✓	✓		✓			
(V2) Operating on a Variable	✓	✓			✓	✓		✓		✓			
(V3) Prediction 1								✓					
(V4) Prediction 2								✓					
(V5) Choosing a Variable Name								✓					
(V6) More than one Variable								✓					
(V7) Creating your own Design	✓	✓	✓		✓	✓		✓		✓			
(V8) A General Circle Procedure	✓		✓		✓		✓	✓		✓			
(V9) General Superprocedures								✓		✓			
(V10) General Superprocedures: Prediction													

	Length	Estimation	Angle	Direction	Decimals	Negative numbers	Scale	Algebra	Geometric transformations	Ratio and proportion	Coordinates	Graphs	Random processes
(T) Turtle Turn and Angle													
(T1) Thinking about Angles			✓										
(T2) Measuring Angles			✓										
(T3) An Angle Bug		✓	✓										
(T4) Creating your own Design	✓		✓										
(T5) Investigating Polygons	✓		✓		✓								
(T6) Investigating Circles	✓		✓		✓								
(A) Arithmetic													
(A1) Calculating with the Computer					✓								
(A2) Using Decimal Numbers	✓				✓	✓		✓					
(A3) Using Negative Numbers	✓				✓	✓		✓					
(A4) Random Numbers													✓
(A5) Random Investigations													✓
(R) Similarity and Proportion													
(R1) In Proportion	✓	✓								✓			
(R2) Hats in Proportion	✓	✓								✓			
(F) Functions													
(F1) Doing and Undoing					✓	✓		✓					
(F2) A Function Machine					✓	✓		✓					
(F3) Guess my Function					✓	✓		✓					
(F4) Undoing a Function					✓	✓		✓					
(F5) Fun with Functions					✓	✓		✓					
(F6) Algebra Expressions – 1					✓	✓		✓					
(F7) Algebra Expressions – 2					✓	✓		✓					
(F8) A Function Investigation								✓					
(F9) A Puzzle								✓					

	Length	Estimation	Angle	Direction	Decimals	Negative numbers	Scale	Algebra	Geometric transformations	Ratio and proportion	Coordinates	Graphs	Random processes
(C) Coordinates and Turtle Heading													
(C1) Coordinates and the Hidden Grid	✓	✓			✓	✓					✓		
(C2) Wallpaper Designs	✓	✓			✓	✓			✓		✓		
(C3) Tile Designs	✓	✓			✓	✓			✓		✓		
(C4) Turtle Heading			✓	✓									
(G) Graphs													
(G1) Coordinates and Graphs						✓		✓			✓	✓	
(G2) Straight Line Graphs						✓		✓			✓	✓	
(TR) Geometrical Transformations													
(TR1) Reflection			✓	✓					✓				
(TR2) Symmetrical Patterns			✓	✓					✓				
(TR3) Rotation			✓	✓					✓				
(RR) Spirals/Recursion													
(RR1) Spirals						✓		✓					
(RR2) Investigating Spirals						✓		✓					
(RR3) Spiral Sequences						✓		✓					

Bibliography

Children learning with Logo

    Author: Katrina Blythe
    Date: 1990
    Publisher: NCET
A valuable account of primary pupils' use of Logo.

Computer science — Logo style (Volumes 1 and 2)

    Author: B Harvey
    Date: 1985
    Publisher: MIT Press, Cambridge, Massachusetts
Serious and accessible books to teach yourself about Logo as a programming
language.

Learning Logo and mathematics

    Authors: C Hoyles and R Noss
    Date: 1991
    Publisher: MIT Press, Cambridge, Massachusetts
A volume of invited contributions on research and curriculum development
in Logo which draws together the first decade of work since *Mindstorms*.

Logo for the Apple II

    Author: H Abelson
    Date: 1982
    Publisher: Byte Books — McGraw Hill
One of the most straightforward 'teach yourself' books — Apple II Logo is
very similar to Logotron Logo.

Logo mathematics in the classroom

    Authors: C Hoyles and R Sutherland
    Date: 1989
    Publisher: Routledge
Based on the Logo Maths Project, this book describes in detail what and
how pupils learn in Logo.

Making Logo work — a guide for teachers

    Authors: Janet Ainley and Ronnie Goldstein
    Date: 1988
    Publisher: Basil Blackwell
A useful work which discusses some of the organisational issues of using
Logo in secondary schools.

Microworlds adventures with Logo

    Author: R Noss, C Smallman and M Thorne
    Date: 1985
    Publisher: Stanley Thornes
A book mainly for children, providing a range of starting points.

Mindstorms – children, computers and powerful ideas

Author: S Papert
Date: 1982
Publisher: The Harvester Press
Essential reading for anyone who wants to find out about the philosophy
and vision behind the early Logo work.

Turtle geometry: the computer as a medium for exploring mathematics

Authors: H Abelson and A di Sessa
Date: 1981
Publisher: MIT Press, Cambridge, Massachusetts
One of the earliest and most important books on mathematics and Logo.
Although many of the ideas presented are challenging it is a wonderful
book to dip into for inspiration. Also many Logo developments (for example
3-D Logo) were influenced by this book.

Visual modelling with Logo: a structural approach to seeing

Author; J Clayson
Date: 1988
Publisher. MIT Press, Cambridge, Massachusetts
A fantastic source of ideas on Logo, geometry and visualisation.

Micromaths

Published by Basil Blackwell Limited, three times a year.
A journal of the Association of Teachers of Mathematics which includes
many valuable articles on using Logo in the classroom. In particular the
Logo Special Issue (Volume 7, Number 1) is well worth reading.

Appendix: Some important differences between Nimbus Logo and Logotron Logo

The most important difference between Logotron Logo for the BBC and the Archimedes Nimbus Logo is the difference in screen scale. One turtle step in Nimbus Logo is approximately four times as big as one turtle step in Logotron Logo. Unfortunately Nimbus have released many difference versions of Logo. They have slowly moved from their early idiosyncratic version of Logo to the more standard and widely available form. This does however mean that the version available in your school may be slightly different from the one used in the Logo materials in this pack. As a teacher you will probably find this very frustrating, but you will be surprised at how confidently pupils deal with these small differences.

Below is a summary of some possible differences but we suggest you add your own notes on differences when you discover them.

● Some earlier versions of Nimbus Logo do not use the command END at the end of a procedure. If this is the case do not add END, because in this version END has another meaning.

● There were many differences in the names of commands in the earlier versions of Nimbus Logo. In the later versions of Nimbus Logo you can often use both the 'old' commands and the 'new' commands. The following are some of the changes:

Old version	Newer versions
RUBBER	PE
LIFT	PU
DROP	PD
BUILD	TO
CHANGE	EDIT

CenturyMATHS

developed at the Institute of Education, University of London

Author: Ros Sutherland
Illustrator: Sharon Perks
Design: Susie Home
Typeset by Action Typesetting
Cover designers: Chris Gilbert and Susie Home
Printed and bound by Martins of Berwick

First published in 1991 by
Stanley Thornes (Publishers) Ltd
Old Station Drive
Leckhampton
Cheltenham GL53 0DN
England

Acknowledgements
Professor Celia Hoyles and Dr Richard Noss, consultants during the development of **Century Maths.**

British Library Cataloguing in Publication Data
LogoPack 1.
  005.13

  ISBN 0 – 7487 – 1160 – 0